On 19 April 1956, in the Cathedral of St Nicholas, Monaco, Grace Patricia Kelly married His Serene Highness Prince Rainier III. To the rest of the world, their wedding was the ultimate version of the classic fairytale. She, the third child of a Philadelphia bricklayer, had left an unhappy home to find fame and fortune in Hollywood. He, the archetypal dashing prince, had transported her across two continents to a palace where they would rule together and live happily ever after. The true story of their love affair is no less remarkable.

Culver Pictures Inc

SEPARATE DESTINIES

IN THE YEAR THAT GRACE WAS BORN IN PHILADELPHIA, YOUNG RAINIER LEFT THE OBSCURE PRINCIPALITY OF MONACO IN SEARCH OF AN EDUCATION. BEFORE 20 YEARS HAD PASSED, SHE WAS ON THE BRINK OF STARDOM, HE WAS THE HEIR APPARENT

O N 12 NOVEMBER 1929, A SECOND daughter and third child was born to John (known as Jack) and Margaret Kelly of Philadelphia. The baby, Grace Patricia Kelly, spent her childhood as an uncomfortable third in a family of four – and last in the affections of both her parents. Her father's favourite was his adored eldest daughter, Margaret – known as Peggy – while he devoted much time and attention to making his only son John, also known as Kell, a chip off the old block. Her mother lavished her love on the baby of the family, Elizabeth Anne – Lizanne – born nearly four years after Grace.

Grace was an awkward little thing, not even very pretty before she became a teenager. In a family that prided itself on its good looks and its reputation for strapping athletes, she was not impressive physically or athletically.

The little princess

Grace's father, John Henry Kelly, was the son of Irish immigrants. His father, also John Henry Kelly, had come from County Mayo in Ireland. Driven by privation and persecution, the senior Kelly had set sail for the New World before he was quite 20. There he married Mary Ann Costello, a strong-willed, hard-working young woman, also an emigrant from Ireland. Ten children were born over the years, Grace's father, John, being the ninth.

Life was hard and the proud Kellys were set to work early, toiling in factories. But the indomitable will of their mother pressed them on. Self-educated, she instilled traditional immigrant values – hard work, discipline, honesty, ambition and patriotism.

Grace's father was an Olympic rowing champion – stunningly handsome and

Culver Pictures Inc

♛ *The Kelly children were all brought up in a grand 17-room house in fashionable Henry Avenue, Philadelphia. The opulent exterior concealed a cold, unloving atmosphere for the young and sickly Grace* above centre *who spent her childhood in the shadow of elder brother John and sister Peggy*

Bulletin/Temple Urban Archives

beautifully built, a catch in all senses for the girls who threw themselves at him. Margaret Majer was his match in every way – she was beautiful, popular and independent.

She modelled for magazines, gained a degree in physical education and had a career as a swimming instructor. Her parents were German, with a more exalted pedigree than that of the Kellys – her grandfather owned a castle and an estate – so she was not going to throw herself away on Jack Kelly just because he asked. It was a full ten years after they first met that she agreed to marry him.

By the time he was 36, Jack Kelly had made enough money from his building contracting business to have a 17-room mansion built. It was here that Grace grew up in a comfortable, middle-class home in Philadelphia. But her parents made no attempt to hide their feelings of favouritism, and the idea within the family was that Grace would never amount to much. She was a sickly child, suffering one minor illness after another, as is often the case with a child who misses the warmth of parental affection.

Neither was there much comfort from her brother and sisters. Kell was not interested in her, Peggy bullied her, and when she, in her turn, tried to bully Lizanne, the bumptious baby of the family simply turned the tables on her.

In compensation, Grace retreated into a world of her own populated by dolls who, unquestioning, obeyed the dictates of her vivid imagination. She loved pretending to be a princess, and 'Princess' became her nickname.

The heir apparent
On the last day of May in 1923, in the Principality of Monaco, the smallest country in the world, the first male heir to the throne for 53 years was born. It could easily be imagined that the baby Prince Rainier III's life was to be charmed – but nothing could be further from the truth. His grandfather, Louis II, had married the daughter of a laundress from Algeria, and Rainier's great-grandfather, Prince Albert, would not recognize her marriage to his son, or their only child, Charlotte, as a rightful heir to the Grimaldi throne.

Decades passed until, nearing death, Albert finally acknowledged that unless he accepted Charlotte's claim to the throne as legitimate, the Grimaldi line would die out. Monaco

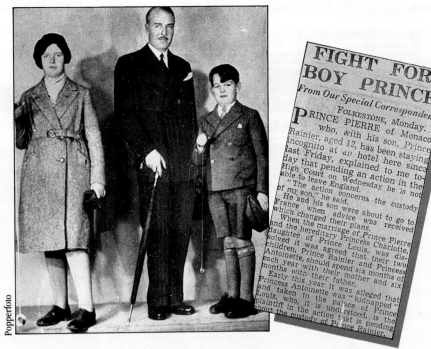

Popperfoto

FIGHT FOR BOY PRINCE

From Our Special Correspondent

FOLKESTONE, Monday.

PRINCE PIERRE of Monaco who, with his son, Prince Rainier, aged 12, has been staying incognito at an hotel here since last Friday, explained to me today that pending an action in the High Court on Wednesday he is not able to leave England.

"The action concerns the custody of my son," he said.

He and his son were about to go to France when advice was received which changed their plans.

When the marriage of Prince Pierre and the hereditary Princess Charlotte, daughter of Prince Louis, was dissolved it was agreed that their two children, Prince Rainier and Princess Antoinette, should spend six months of each year with their mother and six months with their father.

Early this year it was alleged that Princess Antoinette was "kidnapped" and taken to the palace of Prince Louis, who, it is understood, is the plaintiff in the action that is pending about the custody of Prince Rainier.

would then lose its centuries-old autonomy and become absorbed into France.

Charlotte was forced into a 'suitable' arranged marriage with a French nobleman, Comte Pierre de Polignac. The union resulted in a daughter, Princess Antoinette. A year after her father, Prince Louis, succeeded to the throne, Charlotte gave birth to her last child – the new male heir – Prince Rainier.

Some arranged marriages work, but this one was doomed. The infant Prince was soon given into the hands of a traditional English nanny, while his parents lived out what was left of their marriage in an atmosphere of barely concealed hostility.

When he was six years old, Rainier was packed off across the sea to England and the regimented life of an English preparatory school, Summerfields at St Leonard's-on-Sea. From here, he was sent to Stowe, a famous English public school, where he was caned regularly and made to fag for older boys. He was nicknamed 'fat little Monaco'; this made the sensitive child withdraw into his shell and become a shy loner even less likely to attract the friends he wanted desperately.

Meanwhile, his parents' marriage was worsening and, in an acrimonious divorce – doubly scandalous in the royal family of a Catholic country – his father, Pierre, was awarded custody.

When Rainier was 14, his life took a turn for the better. He was moved from Stowe and sent to school in Geneva. The cosmopolitan atmosphere was like a breath of fresh air to a teenager who had spent his early years paying dearly for not being born a little English boy.

'We were always competing. Competing for everything – competing for love'

GRACE KELLY

♛ *Both Rainier right and his sister Antoinette left were victims of the tug of love between their parents, Comte Pierre de Polignac and Princess Charlotte. Pierre centre was awarded custody of the children and took them with him to live in Paris where both were intensely unhappy*

♛ *The main casualty of the divorce was Rainier's mother, Charlotte. To the Monégasques, Charlotte's dubious ancestry and her pro-Fascist sympathies during World War 2 were highly distasteful, encouraging Prince Louis II to name Rainier as his rightful heir and bypass her completely. She eventually settled in Paris with her assortment of dogs, finally dying in 1977*

Popperfoto

The Photographers' Library

3

Culver Pictures Inc

⚜ *Baby Grace, aged 18 months*

Bulletin/Temple Urban Archives

⚜ *Mother and children. Sister Lizanne holds centre stage*

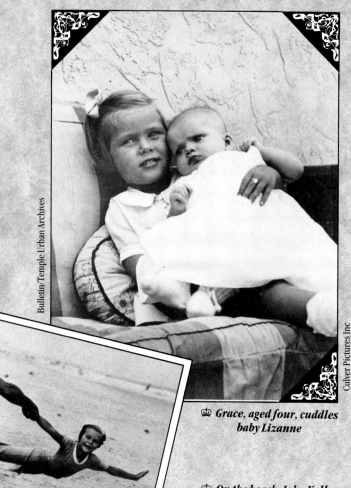

Bulletin/Temple Urban Archives

Culver Pictures Inc

⚜ *Grace, aged four, cuddles baby Lizanne*

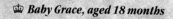

⚜ *On the beach. John Kelly plays with Grace*

⚜ *School days. Grace and Lizanne in party dresses pose for the camera*

♔ *Peggy and Lizanne play the
piano for Kell and Grace*

Bulletin/Temple Urban Archives

UPI/Bettmann Newsphotos

♔ *Antoinette and Rainier in Monégasque
costume at a Palace garden party in 1930*

Bulletin/Temple Urban Archives

♔ *John Kelly and his bathing
beauties, Lizanne* left *and Grace, 17,* right

♔ *1947. Grace pins the Olympic
badge on brother Kell at Henley*

Acme/Temple Urban Archives

♔ *The royal children, 1929, just
before Rainier left for England*

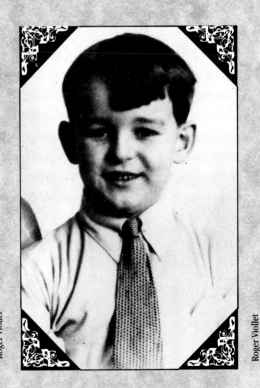

Roger Viollet

♔ *The heir to the throne. The
future Prince Rainier aged six*

Roger Viollet

♛ *Waiting in the wings, the heir apparent watches the Jubilee celebrations in 1947 with his grandfather, Louis II. Also in attendance is Louis's second wife, Princess Ghislaine*

♛ *When in 1949, Louis abdicated due to prolonged illness and died a month later, Rainier finally succeeded to the throne. Aged 26, he was now the most eligible bachelor in Europe* below right

LEAVING CHILDHOOD BEHIND

There was just one word to describe leaving Stowe – 'Wonderful,' was Rainier's verdict. The strict training had paid off, though, for Rainier was a good student and continued to do well. He went on to the École Libre des Sciences Politiques and graduated in 1944.

The actress emerges

By the time Rainier graduated, Grace had begun to find an inner peace and came to terms with her position in the family. The early loneliness and reliance on the artificial world of dolls resulted in an interest in drama that blossomed between the ages of nine and twelve when she joined an amateur dramatics company.

Although her immediate family lived for sport, drama was in Grace's blood. She had been named after an aunt who was an actress and who had died tragically at the age of 22. One uncle, Walter Kelly, was a top vaudeville star, and later a movie actor, and another uncle, George Kelly, was a famous Pulitzer prize-winning playwright. Not only that, Grace had natural talent.

Acting gave Grace confidence and in the next few years, a metamorphosis took place that was almost unnoticed by her family. She had been the plainest of the girls, had a squeaky voice, was rather plump and because she was short-sighted, she had had to wear glasses. But by the time she was 14, she had shot up into a tall and willowy blonde with perfect, even

Topham Picture Library

features, blue-grey eyes and beautiful, fair skin.

An early boyfriend recalled, 'Everyone who took her out fell in love with her.' Even her mother, who tended to be grudging about Grace's charms, had to notice after a while when, as she said, 'Men began proposing to my daughter Grace,' who was then barely 15.

Grace met her first serious boyfriend while at high school when she was 14 and he was 16. Harper Davis was 'a nice clean-cut boy', so her mother said, which also gave him the distinction of being the last boyfriend of whom her family ever approved. Tragically, he became ill with multiple sclerosis when he was 19 and died seven years later.

Starting a career

When Grace graduated from high school, the tacit assumption was that the next step was marriage and life as a wife, mother and home-maker. Meanwhile, as many rich and well-bred Philadelphian girls did, she could mark time by going to college to polish up her mind for her husband-to-be.

♛ *In 1947, watched by the entire Kelly family, Kell won the Diamond Sculls at Henley. Nothing Grace ever achieved was acknowledged by her father*

♛ Below left *When Grace entered the Academy of Dramatic Arts her emergent beauty inspired one director to describe her as 'the kind of girl every man dreams of marrying'*

Grace, however, had other ideas. She had her sights set on the prestigious American Academy of Dramatic Arts in New York — and not simply as a way of marking time. Some of the best moments of her life so far had been on the stage, and she wanted to make it her career.

In 1947, she moved into a select women-only hostel, tightly controlled and chaperoned, and started her studies. Even at the age of 18, Grace was the epitome of the lady, with tai-lored, sensible clothes, hat and veil — and the white gloves that were to become her hall-mark. 'She was terribly sedate,' one of her fel-low students at drama school remembered.

It was the combination of exquisite lady-like control in a girl with perfect natural beauty — glossy hair and barely made-up face — who was neither cold nor unsexy, that was already making men fall at her feet. On one occasion, a family friend arranged for her to be companion to the Shah of Iran when he was in New York for a week. He was clearly smitten by her and showered her with expensive jewellery. He even asked her to marry him, but she turned him down because of her career.

Acting was of paramount importance. Slowly, her troublesome voice was becoming as smooth as 'cream of tomato soup', with more than a trace of an English accent — meanwhile, she was also working as a model. On leaving the Academy, she was immediately taken on by a repertory theatre. A small part in a Hollywood film, *Fourteen Hours*, failed to impress, however, and she resolved to try her luck on Broadway.

7

Culver Pictures Inc

GRACE, THE MODEL

Modelling gave Grace the chance to make some extra money in New York. She may not have been a top model but she was versatile. Her own view, however, was that she was terrible. 'Anyone watching me pitch for Old Gold,' she said, 'would have switched to Camels'

Bulletin/Temple Urban Archives

Inquirer/Temple Urban Archives

Bulletin/Temple Urban Archives

"For a TREAT in
— have a

Old G

Old Gold

As Grace pursued her modelling career, political trouble was brewing in Monaco. Rainier's parents' behaviour had caused problems and concern for the strictly Catholic people of Monaco. Worse still, Charlotte made it clear during the war that she was pro-Mussolini. As Louis grew older, and the time drew near for Charlotte to succeed, she seemed less and less worthy for the task.

So in 1944, Prince Louis took the step of naming his grandson, Rainier, his rightful heir and Crown Prince, thus bypassing Charlotte.

The homecoming

The 21-year-old graduate arrived back in his own country – the place where he had spent so little time – eager now to fulfil his destiny. At his grandfather's side he hoped to learn how to become a great statesman. But Prince Louis had never shown much interest in Monaco and spent as little time there as possible. The Palace was neglected and crumbling away – and so was Monaco's wealth.

Rainier, disappointed and pained for his run-down country, left Monaco and joined the Free French Forces. In his fight against the Nazis, he was awarded the Croix de Guerre and the Bronze Star, and later he became a Chevalier of the Légion d'Honneur.

In 1947, he returned home and found his country was in a worse state than ever, and at the age of 24, he found himself without a clear-cut role; it was not surprising that his interests now took another turn.

Over the next couple of years, tales of Rainier's exploits made colourful reading. His pursuits were manly and dangerous – racing, downhill skiing and hunting.

However, the playboy years were all too short. On 9 May 1949, just three weeks before his 26th birthday, his grandfather died, and he became his Serene Highness Prince Rainier III of Monaco.

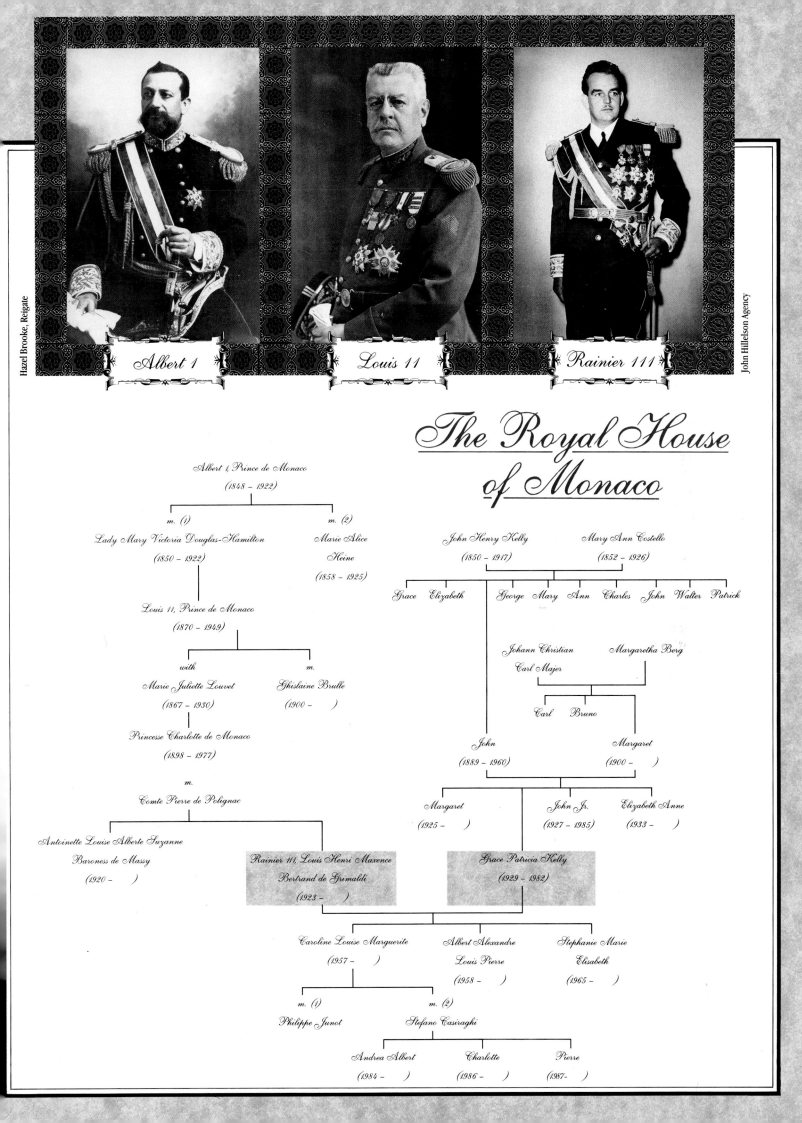

Albert 1   Louis 11   Rainier 111

The Royal House of Monaco

Albert 1, Prince de Monaco
(1848 – 1922)

m. (1)
Lady Mary Victoria Douglas-Hamilton
(1850 – 1922)

m. (2)
Marie Alice Heine
(1858 – 1925)

Louis 11, Prince de Monaco
(1870 – 1949)

with
Marie Juliette Louvet
(1867 – 1930)

m.
Ghislaine Brulle
(1900 –   )

Princesse Charlotte de Monaco
(1898 – 1977)

m.
Comte Pierre de Polignac

Antoinette Louise Alberte Suzanne
Baroness de Massy
(1920 –   )

Rainier 111, Louis Henri Maxence
Bertrand de Grimaldi
(1923 –   )

John Henry Kelly
(1850 – 1917)

Mary Ann Costello
(1852 – 1926)

Grace   Elizabeth   George   Mary   Ann   Charles   John   Walter   Patrick

Johann Christian
Carl Majer

Margaretha Berg

Carl   Bruno

John
(1889 – 1960)

Margaret
(1900 –   )

Margaret
(1925 –   )

John Jr.
(1927 – 1985)

Elizabeth Anne
(1933 –   )

Grace Patricia Kelly
(1929 – 1982)

Caroline Louise Marguerite
(1957 –   )

Albert Alexandre
Louis Pierre
(1958 –   )

Stephanie Marie
Elisabeth
(1965 –   )

m. (1)
Philippe Junot

m. (2)
Stefano Casiraghi

Andrea Albert
(1984 –   )

Charlotte
(1986 –   )

Pierre
(1987 –   )

THE MONÉGASQUE TRADITION

Monaco is a tiny but ancient principality, fiercely independent although forced always to live in the shadow of France. Unfortunately, many irreplaceable royal treasures disappeared after the French Revolution, but the magnificent throne room in the Palais Princier and the picturesque Grimaldi coat of arms are perfect reflections of its turbulent and colourful history

♛ Steeped in symbolism, the Grimaldi coat of arms and the Throne Room in the Royal Palace recall the splendid history of Monaco. The throne *below*, flanked by portraits of earlier princes, is of gold-lacquered wood, surmounted by a rich velvet canopy. The painted ceiling by Genoese artist Orazzio Ferrari dates from the 17th century. The coat of arms *inset* depicts in dramatic form how the Grimaldi dynasty began. Two friars flourish swords over a heraldic shield, surmounted by the royal crown. The motto 'Deo Juvante' means 'With God's help'. The story goes that in 1297, Francesco Grimaldi disguised himself as a friar and, concealing a sword under his habit, succeeded in capturing the fortress from its Genoese occupants. Early Grimaldi coats of arms, dating from 1641, are shown *above*

Magnum

♛ The sash of the Order of St Charles, dating from 1858, was worn for the first time by Princess Grace after her marriage. Other Monégasque orders and distinctions worn here by Rainier include: Ordre du Mérite Culturel, Médaille d'Honneur, Médaille du Travail, Médaille de l'Éducation Physique et des Sports, Médaille de la Reconnaissance de la Croix-Rouge Monégasque. *Right* Grace wears her much loved cameo brooch, a treasured Grimaldi family heirloom

Rex Features

'*It was impossible not to fall in love with Grace*'

WILLIAM HOLDEN

THE PRINCE AND HIGH SOCIETY

John Frost

BY 1952, GRACE WAS ESTABLISHED AS A STAR. YET MUCH OF HER SENSE OF ISOLATION REMAINED, ONLY PARTLY ASSUAGED BY LIAISONS WITH HER LEADING MEN. MEETING RAINIER GAVE HER THE SECURITY SHE CRAVED

I N THE SUMMER OF 1951, A TELEGRAM arrived that would change Grace's life. It read: 'Can you report Aug 28, lead opposite Gary Cooper, tentative title *High Noon*?' Not only was she being asked to play opposite one of Hollywood's foremost stars, but the illustrious production team comprised Stanley Kramer as producer, Fred Zinnemann as director and Carl Foreman as writer. It was the first sign of the luck that was never to desert her during her professional life. Grace was not chosen on the strength of her talent, but on the basis of her looks – in this case, because they were, as the director said, 'straitlaced and virginal', and perfect for the young Quaker bride she was to portray.

High Noon has since become a classic. Gary Cooper won an Oscar but although Grace was shocked by her own performance, which she found wooden and emotionless, this was the very quality that Fred Zinnemann had wanted. And his confidence was borne out by the excellent reviews.

Popperfoto

Popperfoto

Stardom assured

It was Grace's subsequent film that really launched her career. This was *Mogambo*, an adventure film set in Africa, in which she would play opposite one of her great heroes – Clark Gable. So much did she want to do this film that she even agreed to sign a seven-year contract with MGM.

Grace and Gable became fast friends during this film – some said they were lovers. Certainly Gable made it clear that he considered himself 'old enough to be your father', and Grace referred to him as 'Ba' – Swahili for father. But she adored him, and he came to admire her both as an actress and as a woman.

If Gable did not fall in love with his 23-year-old co-star, he was probably her last leading man not to. Already in *Mogambo* the quality that was to captivate men off-screen was becoming apparent on film too. One review read, 'Her particular quality is the suggestion that she is wellborn without being arrogant, cultivated without being stuffy, and highly charged emotionally without appearing to be blatant.'

With Alfred Hitchcock, Grace formed a brilliant actress-and-director relationship. No other director used all her qualities and talents as he did, and no other female star ever again gave him the performances he drew from her. In just over a year, 1954–5, they made *Dial M for Murder*, *Rear Window* and *To Catch*

As Grace's career started to take off, Rainier was involved in a passionate affair with French film star, Gisèle Pascal. He reluctantly finished with her when she failed a fertility test

Syndication International

👑 *Grace and the director Alfred Hitchcock first worked together on the film* Dial M for Murder. *In just over a year, they made three films together and built up a close and successful working relationship. They understood each other well, Hitchcock being the first director to exploit Grace's vibrant and sensual personality, hidden beneath the famously cool exterior*

a Thief. All have proved to be classics.

Grace's cool beauty disturbed Hitchcock personally, but it was the way he could transmute this on to film that revealed his genius. Privately, he would try to ruffle Grace. At one point he persisted in telling vulgar stories to Ray Milland, her co-star in *Dial M for Murder*, in front of Grace. 'He turned to me and said, "Are you shocked, Miss Kelly?" I said, "No, I went to a girl's convent school, Mr Hitchcock, I heard all those things when I was 13."'

Rumours that Grace and her co-star, Ray Milland, who was married, were having an affair ruined the latter part of the filming of *Dial*

M for Murder, and Grace had her first taste of the adverse side of fame in gossip magazines that intrude and cause trouble. It was true that Grace had her romantic involvements, but none that survived the displeasure of her family. She seemed to have the unfortunate gift of picking men that the Kelly clan found quite unsuitable. Once they had made their feelings clear, the romances always petered out.

Grace's most serious personal relationship was with Oleg Cassini, a Russian who was brought up in Florence. They wanted to marry but he was 16 years older than she was, had been twice married and divorced and was also a dedicated womanizer.

Cassini was eventually invited by Grace's family to Philadelphia. The weekend was a disaster and the relationship soon broke up.

But still, men continued to fall for her. In 1954, Grace began filming *Country Girl*, and it is said that both her co-stars, Bing Crosby and William Holden, fell in love with her.

Her part in *Country Girl* was Grace's first and last serious dramatic film role. She played the defeated, down-trodden wife of an alcoholic – and did so with such force that she won the Oscar for best actress in the ceremony on 30 March 1955.

In search of a princess

Grace had managed to fit in a fleeting visit to Monaco while *To Catch a Thief* was filmed on the French Riviera. But she knew little about its Prince, and much less about his country and its troubles.

As soon as Rainier had become ruler of Monaco, he had started a radical re-

HIGH NOON With Gary Cooper/1952

MOGAMBO With Clark Gable/1953

TO CATCH A THIEF With Cary Grant/1955

COUNTRY GIRL With Bing Crosby/195

From left to right: Pictorial Parade, Globe Photos, Rex Features, Pictorial Parade, UPI/Bettmann Newsphotos, Kobal Collection, London

examination of Monaco's economic policy. One of the first things he did was to involve the Greek shipping tycoon, Aristotle Onassis, who had the personal fortune and the business acumen necessary to help restore Monaco.

The playboy Prince, romantically at least, had also settled down. He was deeply involved for a time with a French film star, Gisèle Pascal. Although she did not move into the Palace, Rainier installed her in his Beaulieu villa. There was no official engagement, but his romance with Gisèle was no secret. It was said that the citizens of Monaco considered her to be their uncrowned Princess.

The romance ended in 1953 when Gisèle underwent the necessary fertility test, which she failed. Rainier immediately broke off the relationship. Ironically, Gisèle later married – and bore her husband a child.

By 1955, Rainier was 32 and more than ready to settle down. In an interview published in the American *Collier's Magazine*, he described the problems attached to meeting and getting to know a woman he could love and eventually marry: 'A bachelor's life is lonely, empty, and particularly so for a prince. I cannot behave like an ordinary bachelor. I have no private life. I can not go out without being followed, watched and gossiped about.'

The greatest difficulty, he said, was, 'knowing a girl long and intimately enough ... if *you* met a pretty girl at a party and you were attracted to her and she to you, well, you could say: "What are you doing next Saturday evening?" ... I cannot do that. I have neither the free time nor the privacy.'

But for all that, Rainier had a vision of the kind of girl he wanted to marry. She must, of course, be Catholic as he was, and he was also quite specific about his other requirements. He knew what she should look like: 'a girl who is fair-haired and of light complexion, graceful and feminine'. He wanted her to be 'an intelligent girl, but not an intellectual', five to ten years younger than himself. She needed to know how to cook, but also how to manage servants: 'Servants do not respect you if you are not a competent housekeeper.' But more than anything, Rainier wanted someone he could love: 'I want a wife more than a princess. You can learn to be a prince or princess, but you cannot learn to be a certain kind of human being. You either are or you are not naturally sweet and gentle.' She had to combine domesticity and regal style. But how was Rainier to meet this paragon? In fact he had already done so, probably just a few weeks before the interview was given.

Pictorial Parade

THE OLDER MAN

Grace was very much in love with the older, mature Oleg Cassini whom she met in 1955. They wanted to marry but because he was divorced Grace's parents disapproved, and Grace – reluctantly – gave him up

In the five years between 1951 and 1956, Grace Kelly made a total of 11 films. During this period, she starred opposite some of Hollywood's most attractive leading men, many of whom she became involved with

HIGH SOCIETY With Frank Sinatra/1956

FIRST ENCOUNTER

Sygma/John Hillelson

Grace's first meeting with Prince Rainier almost did not happen. At the time, everything seemed to conspire against it, and Grace herself wished more than once that it could be cancelled.

Early in March 1955 – when Grace had been nominated for an Oscar for her role in *Country Girl*, but before the May ceremony – she was invited to be guest of honour at the Cannes Film Festival. It was said that she was invited because every man in France was in love with her. What is more likely is that they wanted her to attend because she was unquestionably the biggest star of the time.

Grace, however, was reluctant. She had just moved into an apartment in New York, and she did not fancy the upheaval of going to France. But pressure was put on her. Eric Johnston, head of the Motion Picture Association of America, told her that she should consider that she would be representing America – a shrewd handling of Grace's temperament and innate sense of duty.

The morning after Grace reached Cannes, she was faced with an impossible schedule. The editor of the French magazine, *Paris Match*, wanted to do a cover story on a meeting between the Hollywood princess and the European Prince Rainier of Monaco.

It was something of a *fait accompli*. The meeting would be at 3.00 pm that afternoon, and Monaco was an hour's drive away. But Grace was faced with a series of practical problems. Firstly, she had nothing to wear. Her suitcase had not been unpacked, and was full of crushed clothes that needed pressing – but there was an electricity strike, so nothing could be done about it. The lack of electrical power also meant that, although she had washed her hair, there was no means of styling it.

On top of everything else, Grace had to be back in Cannes to act as hostess at a reception at 5.30 that same afternoon.

Grace's immediate reaction was that she wanted to cancel the meeting with Rainier, but as she said, 'You can't keep someone like the Prince of Monaco waiting.'

It was a case of make-do-and-mend. Grace fished out the one dress from her case that had suffered least. It had a black cotton satin background against which flourished a large design of red and green cabbage roses – hardly the kind of thing for an intimate meeting with a prince. She solved the problem of her hair by twisting it into a chignon and, in the absence of

Pictorial Parade

♔ *When Grace and Rainier met in December 1955, the sheer magnetism between them was noticed by all of Grace's family. The arranged meeting in Monaco started off badly. She had nothing to wear and he turned up late. Nevertheless, in the short time they did have together it was obvious they got on well. The affair was ready to take off*

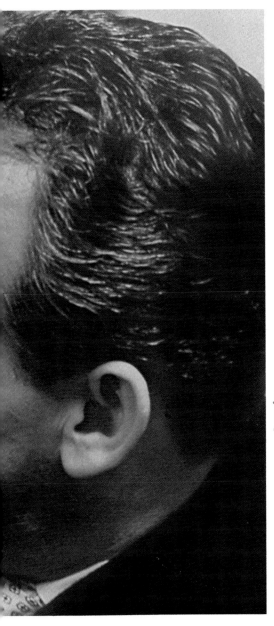

Popperfoto

Bulletin/Temple Urban Archives

👑 *On 5 January 1956, the Kelly family went out for lunch at the Philadelphia Country Club. On their return, they called a press conference at their home to announce the engagement of Grace and Rainier to the world. Mercilessly questioned by the teeming journalists, the couple tried to keep their composure as they kept showing Grace's ring*

👑 *When Rainier came to visit Grace at her family home, he brought his close confidant, Father Tucker. The priest had advised the Prince from an early age and had been the 'matchmaker' in bringing the couple together again*

Topham Picture Library

a hat (needed for meeting a prince), wore a headband decorated with artificial flowers.

But after all, this was work. Grace, the true professional, was shown around the Palace while the *Paris Match* photographers took pictures. By 3.45, however, Grace had had enough. 'I think he is very rude to keep us waiting like this,' she said. 'Let's get out of here.' But before she could manage to leave, Rainier appeared at the door.

The Prince meets his match

Grace had not known what to expect. She only knew about Rainier what she had gleaned during her short time at the Palace. What she saw was a good-looking young man, slightly shorter than herself, with penetrating dark blue eyes and the continental style and manners she had found so irresistible in Oleg Cassini. Previously, Grace had been drawn to older men but this man, only six years older, had the aura of power natural to one who was born to rule. It was a winning formula.

Rainier knew more about the beautiful young actress than she knew about him, but he was unprepared for her personality – shy, unshowy, yet serenely contained.

As Grace had already seen the Palace, Rainier took her around the grounds and showed her his private zoo. They chatted, but only for a short while because Grace had to leave for the next engagement. It was long enough, however, for Rainier to tell Grace that he would be in America that winter, and would very much like to see her again.

The editor from *Paris Match* later recalled, 'We felt like indiscreet onlookers. Grace's complexion seemed to acquire a new glow.' But Grace would not be drawn about the meeting afterwards. All she was prepared to concede was that the Prince was 'charming'.

That Rainier was more than slightly interested was undeniable. Grace was just the kind of girl he had been looking for. He confided this to his spiritual adviser, Father Francis Tucker, who, coincidentally, was also an Irish-

American originally from Philadelphia. He then elected to act as a matchmaker. Father Tucker, Rainier has since said, was very pleased and helpful. Grace was a lovely Catholic girl, from a good family and of the right age.

A courtship arranged

Although Grace was obviously taken with Prince Rainier, this did not stop her renewing her friendship with a former lover, the French actor Jean-Pierre Aumont. Reporters took pictures of them eating intimately in an out-of-the-way restaurant and soon everybody knew about their romance. It was not to last, however, as the distance between their countries was too great for the relationship to survive.

Father Tucker's chance to matchmake came in the summer. Old friends of the Kellys – Russell and Edie Austin – had tried to get tickets for the Red Cross Gala while touring Monaco but failed. Knowing that Grace had met the Prince, they rang the Palace and asked if there was a chance of Rainier procuring some tickets for them.

Rainier immediately did so, and more. Father Tucker summoned them to the Palace and, during a pleasant meeting, extracted a promise from them in return – a meeting between Grace and Rainier when he went to the United States.

Together at last

Rainier's trip was planned for December. Father Tucker wrote to the Austins and asked them to arrange for the Prince to see the Kellys on Christmas Eve. Rainier would be bringing Father Tucker, and a young doctor, Dr Donat. The Austins' only worry was that Grace might not be nice to Rainier. 'Grace could give anyone the cold shoulder,' they feared. The message was conveyed that, quite the opposite, Grace would like to see the Prince. Years later, she confessed, 'I almost knew I was in love with the Prince before we met for the second time.'

Although Grace made a point of saying that she had not heard from the Prince since they had first met, in fact he had been in touch with her. Through letters and phone calls they had begun to know each other.

Not surprisingly, Grace was nervous. She asked her elder sister, Peggy, to be sure to be there on Christmas Eve 1955 to give her moral support. But Peggy saw that the moment the two met, there were 'sparks flying' between them.

It was a traditional Christmas Eve party, with little time for Rainier and Grace to be by themselves. But Peggy had invited Rainier and his entourage to stay with her, and afterwards

Popperfoto

THE ENGAGEMENT PARTY

As soon as Grace and Rainier's engagement was announced, they came under continuous scrutiny from the American press, particularly so at their glamorous and extravagant engagement party held on 10 January 1956 at New York's Waldorf-Astoria Hotel. At every opportunity, a picture was taken of the happy couple embracing or talking intimately to each other. Rainier found this difficult to handle, particularly as all the attention was focused on Grace – he was considered a mere incidental. Newspapers even candidly printed: 'Not good enough for a Kelly.'

The couple's whirlwind three-week courtship was a great surprise to everyone. Very few people knew that the couple had been secretly corresponding and talking on the phone since their first meeting in the spring of 1955. Grace, in fact, knew that Rainier was seriously contemplating marriage before he came to visit her at Christmas.

Becoming engaged to royalty is never a simple matter, though, as Grace came to find out. It was rumoured that before the engagement was announced, she, like the Prince's former girlfriend, Gisèle Pascal, had to undergo a fertility test to be

Topham Picture Library

Magnum

Pictorial Parade

Magnum

performed by Dr Donat to prove that she could have children and produce the necessary heir for Monaco. Jack Kelly had also been persuaded by Father Tucker to give the Prince a dowry, estimated at around two million dollars. At first, Kelly was outraged by the idea that he should have to pay someone money to marry his daughter. But he was told that this was the usual European royal custom and that the money was a good investment in Monaco's real estate.

In fact, the dowry was needed immediately to help solve the country's short-term cash problems

Grace went with them over to Peggy's where they played cards into the small hours.

The next day, Grace and Rainier went for a drive together, the first time they had ever been truly alone. When they returned, Grace was wearing a 'friendship ring' of gold, studded with diamonds and rubies.

Typically, Jack Kelly was not pleased. Contrary to what might have been expected, he was not over-impressed that Grace's new suitor was a Prince, however charming.

Frankly, Jack Kelly was suspicious of Rainier's motives, and he was blunt about telling his worries to Father Tucker: 'I said I didn't want any damn broken-down Prince who was head of a country over there that nobody knew anything about to marry my daughter.' But Father Tucker was able to reassure him.

On 28 December, Grace had to return to New York to start singing lessons for her next film, *High Society*. Until then, she saw Rainier every day, and he drove her back to New York with Dr Donat. On the morning of 29 December, Grace rang her mother to say that they were 'very much in love' – something that was, by then, quite apparent – and that the Prince had proposed to her. Father Tucker was sent to offer the Prince's formal proposal to Grace's father. The Kellys, now excited about the union, telephoned through their acceptance to Rainier and, on New Year's Eve, the couple were engaged.

The public announcement of the engagement did not come until a few days later, on 5 January 1956, and that was when Rainier first understood the real implications of his proposal. As far as the American press was concerned this was big news, but not because a prince from an obscure little country in Europe was getting married. Where Rainier came from and his royal pedigree were only incidental to the story of Grace Kelly, film star.

For the time being, Grace was letting it be known that she planned to continue as an actress. But Rainier clearly had other plans. He was quoted as saying, 'I don't want my wife to work. She thinks I am right that she should end her film career.'

It was inevitable that Rainier would win – and not surprising that Grace let him. Although being a big star was one of her ambitions, her most cherished one – that of being a star on Broadway, respected for her acting – looked unlikely to materialize. She informed MGM, to whom she was still under contract, that she would be unable to fulfil it. They were gracious – but at a price: the exclusive film rights to the wedding of the century, planned for the April of that year.

LE PALAIS PRINCIER

Perched high above the town of Monte Carlo and standing on the site of a 13th-century fortress is the Palais Princier, home of the Monégasque royal family since the 17th century. Over the years, successive monarchs enlarged and enriched the original buildings, adding galleries and many works of art. In 1956, Princess Grace brought her own special glamour to the Palace and did much to beautify both the interior and the gardens

Spectrum

Robert Harding Picture Library

Frank Spooner

Frank Spooner

👑 The palace stands in a commanding position, overlooking the town of Monte Carlo on one side and the sea on the other. The great doorway *left* is surmounted by a pediment bearing the princely arms. Each day at noon, the traditional ceremony of the changing of the guard takes place in front of the palace entrance *far left*. The Court of Honour *below* is surrounded by an arcaded gallery. It is here that the Monégasque people flock on historic occasions. It provides a beautiful setting for orchestral concerts during the summer. The great double staircase of Carrara marble was inspired by the Horseshoe Staircase at the Chateau of Fontainebleau, near Paris

Camera Press

The rich and sombre decoration of the Louis XV Drawing Room, or Blue State Room, provides a perfect background for the magnificent paintings that line its walls. These include 'The Triumph of Galateus', attributed to the Bolognese artist, Annibale Carracci, and a portrait presented by King Louis XV of France to Antoine I of Monaco. Among some delightful children's portraits are those of Charlotte and Honoré Grimaldi and a picture of an earlier Princess Caroline, painted in 1878. *Left* Princess Grace stands beside a charming little 18th century painting of the French school, representing Spring

Magnum

👑 When she refurbished the private wing of the royal apartments, Princess Grace brought a breath of fresh air into its dusty rooms. *Below* A perfect place for relaxation, the brilliant Mediterranean sun is filtered by sunblinds. Light cane furniture, an aviary and a fine collection of plants complete the picture. *Below right* Uncluttered modern furnishings with low, comfortable seating in plain cream fabric bring a more homely dimension to the palatial proportions of Grace and Rainier's family sitting-room. *Right* The splendid Imperial Drawing Room is decorated in white and gold, with apricot drapery. This room is used for public entertaining. The stunning chandelier which can just be glimpsed is of Venetian crystal, and for candles only. Lighting is provided by lamps around the walls

Sygma/John Hillelson

CROWN MATRIMONIAL

THE WEDDING TOOK PLACE AMID SCENES WHICH BORDERED ON HYSTERIA. THE MONÉGASQUES, THE WORLD'S MEDIA AND THEIR AUDIENCES WERE JUBILANT. THE COUPLE FOUND IT AN ALMOST UNBEARABLE STRAIN

O N 4 APRIL 1956, Grace Kelly set sail on the *SS Constitution* for the eight-day trip that would take her to Monaco and a reunion with her Prince.

With her travelled 72 members of her family and friends and – a last-minute concession – a few selected photographers and reporters. Inevitably, she had a mountain of luggage, consisting of four large trunks and 56 other assorted cases and hatboxes. Most important of these was a steel coffin-type box which contained her sumptuous wedding dress, one of the many gifts to her from MGM studios, and designed by their chief designer, Helen Rose. Inside the suitcases was a wardrobe fit for a princess – a carefully chosen trousseau with clothes by some of the world's top designers, as well as all the clothes she had worn in *High Society* (another gift from MGM).

Rainier set out to meet her in his yacht *Deo Juvante II*, his wedding present to Grace. She waved to him from the deck, and he saluted in return. He brought the yacht alongside and, carrying her pet poodle, Oliver, she descended the gangplank to join him. It was then, perhaps, that Grace first realized that things were to be very different now. For this was no lover's reunion, but a formal, public welcoming of her to Monaco. Grace put out her hand to Rainier and he clasped it in a handshake – there was no kiss, hug or any other intimate gesture of love.

But in every other way it was a delightful welcome. As the yacht neared the shore,

Popperfoto

👑 *Grace left New York like the royalty she was shortly to become. Bands played, sirens sounded and several hundred reporters jostled with Grace's 72 companions for her attention. Somehow she found peace to read Rainier's letters*

Aristotle Onassis had his seaplane drop thousands of red and white carnations – the colours of Monaco – on to the couple in the yacht, most of the flowers landing on the sea, and bobbing along in their wake. The *Constitution* saluted Grace and Rainier with cannon fire, and every other vessel in the harbour added to the noise by sounding their sirens and tooting horns.

On the shore, thousands of people cheered and waved as the couple got into the Prince's green Chrysler for the drive to the Palace. The road was lined with more cheering crowds, all trying to catch their first live glimpse of their new Princess.

Rainier had wanted to make their wedding memorable. But the festivities were to become a nightmare to Grace and Rainier because of the hysterical attention of the world's press.

The situation was truly terrifying. The 1500 or so reporters and photographers outnumbered the invited guests by three to one, and most of them were in no mood to be pleasant. Each and every reporter was looking for a scoop, a story or an angle and, in the absence of hard news, they dished dirt.

It is not hard to imagine the effect of all this on the Royal couple. To find themselves dogged and jostled wherever they went was bad enough, but the fact that the intent was malicious made it very much worse. The effect on Grace was obvious. Although she still looked beautiful, dark circles were starting to appear under her eyes and she was losing weight.

Bulletin/Temple Urban Archives

Popperfoto

WEDDING OF THE CENTURY

On the morning of 18 April 1956, the couple took part in the first marriage ceremony, a civil affair required by law, in the Throne Room of the Palace. Rainier said afterwards, 'By the time the ceremonies started, I was a nervous wreck.' It was true that they both looked tense and strained as this necessary, but emotionally meaningless, ceremony took place.

Grace was dressed in a dress of soft rose Alençon lace, with a Juliet cap in her head. Rainier was dressed formally in a black morning coat. The ceremony was conducted by Monsieur Marcel Portanier, President of the Monaco Council. Behind them sat only a select one hundred guests, as the Throne Room was too small to accommodate them all. Overhead blazed the television arc lights, and the in-

UPI/Bettmann Newsphotos

Gamma/Frank Spooner

trusive eyes of the cameras were fastened on them as the ceremony progressed.

Later, Grace and Rainier threw a huge reception in the courtyard of the Palace for 3000 of the citizens of Monaco.

After the ceremony, Grace joked that she was 'half-married'. Not in the eyes of God though. Yet again the couple spent the night separately – Grace in her rooms at the Palace, Rainier at his villa.

The religious ceremony

The 'real' wedding took place the next day, in the Cathedral of St Nicholas.

The scene was magical. Inside the white stone Gothic church, candles illuminated the high altar, and banks of white flowers cascaded everywhere – even overhead in golden baskets fixed to the chandeliers. The 600 guests included the stars who had become some of Grace's closest friends – Ava Gardner, Gloria Swanson, David Niven and his wife and Cary Grant with his wife were among those present.

♛ *Rehearsed and ready. From the invitations being sent out, to going away on their honeymoon, nothing was left to chance. The flower girls and bridesmaids knew their parts every bit as well as the bride and groom*

Sygma/John Hillelson

Gamma/Frank Spooner

WEDDING FEVER

The wedding of Grace and Rainier was preceded by seven days of non-stop activity – a whirlwind timetable of private and public engagements. Three miles of red carpet wound their way through the streets of Monaco, champagne was virtually on tap, and a host of festivities was sensitively planned and chosen.

High spots included performances by Margot Fonteyn and other ballet stars at the Opera House, a romantic eve-of-ceremony serenade, and a breathtaking midnight firework display. To some people, however, Monaco was more like a battleground, as pickpockets and thieves mingled among the crowds, and Rainier was appalled at the extensive scale of jewel robberies that took place.

Amongst the flurry of activity: *From the top* printing souvenir postcards for the wedding – 350,000 were issued; special commemorative stamps for the occasion; gifts and greetings. *Left* Monégasque sculptor, Ange Zagioni, applies finishing touches to plaster figurines which were cast in sugar to decorate the royal wedding cake

According to Monégasque tradition, Grace had to arrive at the altar first, and she looked stunningly beautiful as she was escorted down the aisle by her father. As she took her place at the altar facing Monaco's bishop, Monsignor Gilles Barthe, a fanfare of trumpets announced that Rainier had arrived, and it was only then that Jack Kelly left his daughter's side to take his seat next to his wife.

The bride and bridesmaids

Grace had been followed by four little flower girls who wore demure little dresses made of white Swiss broderie anglaise.

The bridesmaids, including Peggy as maid of honour and six of Grace's friends, stood behind her at the altar. They, like the bride, were in dresses designed by Helen Rose. Both groups watched shyly as the service got under way.

As the ceremony progressed, Grace and Rainier knelt on golden stools, holding hands before Monsignor Barthe. They looked intent on what was happening, seemingly oblivious of the television crews and 600 guests ranged in the seats behind them. But, as Rainier was to say, the reporters and cameras reduced the dignity of the occasion: 'We both agreed that we should really have got married in a little chapel in the mountains.'

Man and wife

Finally, the bishop said, 'I declare you united in marriage in the name of the Father, the Son and the Holy Ghost' and, at the words, the white-suited six-year-old page, Sebastien von Fursten-berg, brought them their wedding rings on a silver salver. Rainier fumbled as he placed the ring on Grace's finger, and she had to help him, but his own ring slipped smoothly on. At no point in the ceremony did they kiss.

But there was no doubt as they left the cathedral that they were a couple in love who had survived an ordeal. Grace was smiling irrepressibly, and she made Rainier laugh.

Holding hands, they climbed into their open-topped Rolls (a wedding gift from the people of Monaco) which drove them through the streets, flanked by a motorcycle escort, to a tiny harbourside church. The final religious ceremony was for Grace alone. She had to lay her bouquet at a wooden altar bearing a statue of Monaco's patron saint, St Dévote – a young girl who had been martyred 1600 years before – and ask her to bless the marriage.

Back at the Palace in the courtyard another wedding reception was laid on – this time only for the 600 guests. The wedding cake was an enormous five-tier confection, taller than the bride and groom.

Sygma/John Hillelson

Syndication International

As the festivities continued, Rainier and Grace slipped away, leaving their guests enjoying themselves. They boarded their yacht and waved to the assembled crowd. Two rockets were shot into the air and, as they soared into the sky, dropped two huge flags — one of Monaco and the other of the United States.

Alone at last

As the yacht sailed out of sight, the strain finally told. The newly-wed couple flopped into two deckchairs and fell instantly asleep. Grace, especially, was exhausted. Slim before she had set out for Monaco, the anxieties of the last few days had caused her to lose ten pounds in weight. Rainier was ever after to refer to the wedding as a 'disastrous affair' and said how disheartened he and Grace had been by the unrelenting pressure of the media and the lack of 'intimacy, solitude and dignity'.

Finally, the couple were alone, except for the discreetly hand-picked crew. They had seven glorious weeks in front of them, with nothing to think of but each other and a blissful honeymoon.

Ironically, and not surprisingly, within a day of leaving Monaco Grace went down with 'flu. But a week later she was fine and they were truly able to enjoy themselves.

The honeymoon was a long leisurely cruise. It took them along the Riviera, to the Balearic Islands, and around the coasts of France and Spain. They were able to touch shore wherever they wanted. The beaches of Corsica were particularly blissful, and they had expanses of white sand all to themselves.

Only one incident marred the honeymoon and reminded them that they were not private citizens but world property. Rainier told of it afterwards: 'An English tourist walked up and calmly stepped between us while his wife took motion pictures. The lady then looked up and blandly requested us to remove our sunglasses so she could get better shots.'

♛ *Grace and Rainier finally escaped when they boarded the royal yacht for their seven-week honeymoon. As they sailed the Mediterranean, the media continued to celebrate. Picture Post was only one of many publications to produce a commemorative issue*

John Frost

THE KELLY LOOK

Grace Kelly was a natural for her greatest true-life role – that of a princess. From her schooldays in Philadelphia to award-winning stardom, she knew instinctively how to carry off a style. Perfectly dressed on State occasions she, equally, did not hesitate to appear in flat shoes or glasses if these suited a particular mood. The epitome of fashion in the early 'fifties, Grace Kelly was no Hollywood sweater girl. Her ideal was that of elegance. From casual sportswear to grand ball-gowns, the look is always ladylike

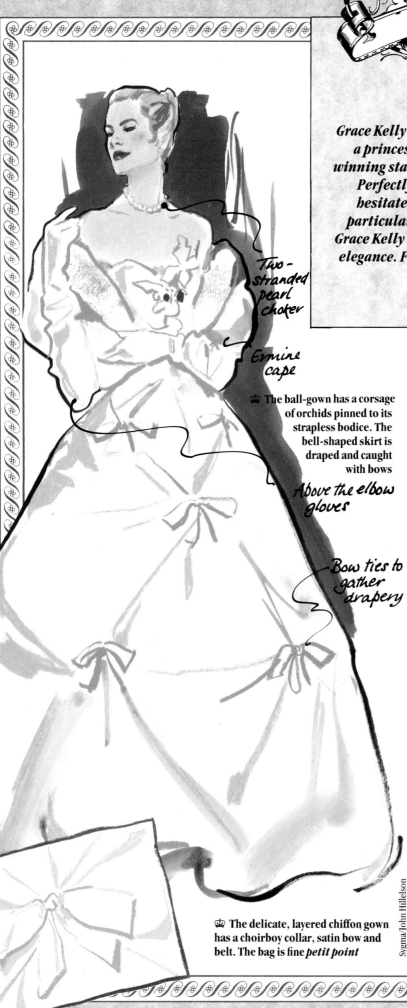

Two-stranded pearl choker

Ermine cape

♛ The ball-gown has a corsage of orchids pinned to its strapless bodice. The bell-shaped skirt is draped and caught with bows

Above the elbow gloves

Bow ties to gather drapery

♛ The delicate, layered chiffon gown has a choirboy collar, satin bow and belt. The bag is fine *petit point*

Sygma/John Hillelson

Lace Juliet cap

Pearl-buttoned bodice

Rose-point lace and seed pearls

Pearl-buttoned cuffs

Deep lace edging

♛ The wedding veil rests on a Juliet cap with a small wreath of tiny orange blossom

Order of St. Charles, Croix de Guerre and Légion d'Honneur

♛ 25 yards of ivory silk taffeta, 100 yards of silk net and 300 yards of Valenciennes lace went into this dream wedding gown, created by Hollywood designer Helen Rose. The fitted lace bodice, buttoned from neck to waist, is sewn with seed pearls, and contrasts with the wide sweeping skirt

♛ Prince Rainier's uniform, which he designed himself, is based on one worn by Napoleon Bonaparte, and features a navy blue tunic and sky blue trousers, banded with gold

Blue bows on three petticoats

Broderie anglaise crown with organza brim

Woven straw hat

♛ The large-brimmed shady straw hat was worn by Grace Kelly when she arrived for her wedding. It was criticized for hiding her face too much

♛ The off-the-face style trimmed with a flyaway bow is in more conventional royal style

Contrasta detachab skirt

Kobal Collection

♛ A typical 'dressmaker' suit of the 'fifties, this single-breasted jacket has soft unstructured lines, unpadded shoulders, a fitted waist and gently flared skirt

♛ Casual wear with a sophisticated look. The halter-necked bodice and tight, cropped trews are topped by a swinging overskirt

Cork-soled mules

♛ In this MGM publicity still, Grace wears a bang-up-to-the-minute ballgown in shaded net. The strapless petal bodice is cinched by a tight, beaded waistline, over a wide crinoline skirt

Contrasting top in silk jersey

♛ The long-sleeved, tight-waisted top over a spreading chiffon skirt is hand-painted with a riot of California poppies in shades of blue

Co·ordinating stripes trim the jacket

Flowers hand-painted on to chiffon fabric

♛ *Left* A casual sports outfit is typical of the American 'college girl' look that suited Grace to perfection

Rex Features

A ROYAL FAMILY

AFTER THEIR WHIRLWIND ROMANCE, GRACE AND RAINIER AT LAST HAD TIME TO GET TO KNOW EACH OTHER PROPERLY. BUT DESPITE THE FULFILMENT OF MOTHERHOOD, GRACE BEGAN TO GROW LONELY

Sygma/John Hillelson

⚜ *The birth of Princess Caroline in January 1957 was a momentous occasion in the lives of Grace and Rainier. Politically, a successor to the throne was ensured, but on a more personal level the birth fulfilled Grace's deepest need – to be a mother*

BY THE TIME THE COUPLE HAD RETURNED to Monaco from their honeymoon, Grace's suspicions were confirmed – she was pregnant. She could hardly doubt it as her symptoms were so strong. 'They told me about morning sickness,' she said ruefully, 'but they didn't tell me you could be sick all day, every day.'

But Grace was affected by more than the usual symptoms. She was unwell throughout her pregnancy with a series of minor complaints such as sore throats and colds, and it did not help that this first pregnancy came at a time of massive adjustment.

For Rainier, who had spent the last seven weeks on holiday, and the few weeks before that wrapped up in wedding preparations, it was essential to get back to real work. Grace now found herself left very much to her own devices – something she did not find easy. She was in a strange country, far from home with no one she could talk to, and – for the first time that she could remember – had nothing to do.

Everything was different for Grace. As she said later, 'At first I thought I wouldn't be able to cope. The biggest change in my life wasn't the Palace. It was the adjustment to marriage itself. I lived alone in New York and in California, and the entire schedule of my life centred around my work. I had to get to the studio on time. I had to arrange my own meals to fit my schedule. My career was the central focus of everything I did. Now my life centred on my husband.'

Grace had always enjoyed her friendships and been a good friend herself. One of the hardest things for her now was to be cut off from her girlfriends, especially when she had so much time and so little to fill it.

Recognizing that Grace needed a companion, Rainier appointed Madge Tivey-Faucon – a woman he had known through his former love, Gisèle Pascal – to be Grace's lady-in-waiting and to teach her French. Madge was also about the same age as Grace, which he felt would be an added advantage. But a member of staff is not a friend, and 'Tiv', as she came to be called, later said that it took her a while to like Grace, whom she clearly despised as being an American and definitely not an aristocrat.

In fact, Grace was not very popular anywhere. The servants in the Palace were resistant to her new authority, and because her

> ## *'The biggest change in my life wasn't the Palace. It was the adjustment to marriage itself'*
> ### PRINCESS GRACE

French was still very poor, she was usually silent in public and embarrassed. The Monégasques interpreted her shy manner as 'icy reserve' and because of this were disappointed in their Princess.

Another difficult adjustment was that Grace had to learn all over again how to behave. As a film star she could be gloriously herself, but as a Princess of Monaco she had to obey the rules laid down for her. She always had to wear a hat at public functions, never step out of the Palace without Rainier or a lady-in-waiting, sign herself Grace de Monaco – even in private correspondence, be curtsied to by all women, and always be referred to as 'Your Highness'.

In September 1956, Grace and Rainier went on a short visit to the United States. Grace was able to visit friends and indulge herself buying baby clothes. But it was rather different returning to her homeland as a Princess – the couple were formally entertained by President Eisenhower, and, inevitably, were dogged by reporters wherever they went. Other official trips were to follow – to Rome in 1957, Paris in 1959 and Ireland in 1961. And always, the press and crowds were there.

At Christmas, Grace presided over a party that she was to throw each Christmas thereafter. She invited every single Monégasque child between the ages of three and twelve to the Palace, without their parents, for a celebration. She entertained the hundreds of children in four shifts and, with her genius for parties, they had a wonderful time.

As the birth grew near, Grace began to prepare herself seriously for motherhood. She read everything she could lay her hands on about natural childbirth and breastfeeding.

In true Grimaldi tradition, it was decided that an heir to the throne should be born at home, and the library in the royal quarters was converted into a delivery room – a disappointment for the many reporters, who had descended vulture-like on Monaco, hoping for a hospital birth so that they could pick up 'stories' from the staff.

Caroline Louise Marguerite was born on 23 January 1957 at 9.27 am, weighing 8lb 3oz. Immediately, a cyclist pedalled to the harbour to give the news to the men manning the cannon on the waterfront, which then blasted 21 times – the traditional message to Monaco that

🔖 *The 1957 visit to Rome where they met Pope Pius XII excited a great deal of publicity. Rainier's displeasure at being photographed is clearly visible – the photographer was later removed from the restaurant by the police*

a girl child had been born. By way of celebration, a national holiday was declared and the only prisoner in Monaco's jail was pardoned and freed.

The joy of motherhood

There was no doubt that Grace was a natural mother. She had always loved children and longed for babies of her own, and the reality did not disappoint her. Nevertheless, it was hard on her that less than five months later she was pregnant again. For, as became standard during Grace's pregnancies, her health suffered.

On 14 March 1958, Albert Alexandre Louis Pierre was born, weighing 8lb 11oz. Rainier was delighted. Although he could be succeeded by a female heir, he had hoped for a boy, and his pleasure was mirrored everywhere in Monaco.

One of the Palace staff broke with protocol and shouted the news to the crowd waiting below. Aristotle Onassis, who was in London at the time, had asked to be called when the baby was born. At the other end of the phone he listened to the cannon fire, and the moment 22 shots had rung out he hung up, knowing that a boy had been born. In the event of a son and heir to the throne of Monaco, the cannon fires 101 times.

Grace was sure of what she wanted from motherhood. 'I'm not going to let public life or anything else push me out of my job as a mother,' she said in an interview. 'In America, children of wealthy parents are so often given over completely to nurses from the start. Mine are not going to be.' In this, she had the full backing of Rainier who was all too familiar with the miseries of an unhappy childhood spent with distant nurses. Grace did have some help, however, first from Margaret Stahl, a maternity nurse from Switzerland, and then, after 'Albie' was born, from Maureen King, an English girl who spoke perfect French.

BIRTH OF AN HEIR

Albert's arrival provided the long-awaited male heir, and caused general rejoicing in Monaco. He was presented to the Monégasques from the Palace balcony with sister Caroline and, on the eve of his christening, the whole Principality was illuminated by a spectacular firework display

LIFE AT THE PALACE

G race was concerned that her children should be brought up as normally as possible, in spite of their royal status. When Caroline reached the age of four, Grace started a class in the Palace so that she could take her lessons with other Monégasque children, and a year later Albert joined the classes with boys of his own age. The children were never allowed to be grand, or get above themselves. Grace was severe with them whenever they showed signs of taking the servants for granted, for example. On one occasion, young Albert was heard to order the butler to take his plate away, so Grace made him do it himself. 'I don't think they realized they were anything special for a long time,' Maureen King was to say.

A royal routine

Life in these early years followed a fairly regular pattern. Grace and Rainier would usually get up at about 8.30 am, and have breakfast in their private dining room with Caroline, Albert and Maureen King. After breakfast, Grace was helped to dress by her English maid and would then go to the library to consult with her staff about menus and the day's events at the Palace. After that she would go to the nursery to play with the children. The family would take a long, leisurely lunch together – normally a formal occasion, with footmen in attendance.

In the afternoon, Grace usually had meetings to attend with the several organizations she was involved with, or she would see people in her private office. Late afternoons were generally spent with the children and Rainier.

Some time after this the children would say goodnight, and a little later Grace would go and tuck them in, read them a story and say their prayers with them. At around nine, she and Rainier would have their evening meal – sometimes with a few guests, occasionally a formal dinner, but often on their own. After dinner, they might go into the garden or have a dip in the pool that Grace had had built.

That was how life was led from November to May, except when they went to ski in Switzerland, or spring shopping in Paris. During the summer the whole family would go to Roc Agel, their retreat – a charming Provençal farmhouse, set on Mont Agel, looking down on Monaco.

Rex Features

It all appeared idyllic, and Grace had times when she was content. But under the surface there were strains, and she was often unhappy – and very lonely. Although she had plenty of visitors, she found it very difficult to meet and make friends in Monaco.

The lonely Princess

True, she was slowly carving out a role for herself in Monaco, but it was many more years before that role was truly defined. She became President of the Monégasque Red Cross, supervised the refurbishing of the hospital, which was renamed after her, and also began to use her influence subtly on her husband as

♔ *As Caroline and Albert grew older, life at home followed a predictable and orderly routine. Rainier, a devoted father, spent as much time as was possible with his children, but work kept him away from his family for long periods. Grace found motherhood fulfilling, but only up to a point, and the loneliness that she felt in a foreign country meant that there were periods when she was far from happy*

Topham Picture Library

Prince. One of her greatest successes was to convince him to introduce votes for women.

Unhappy events

The solitary side of Grace also found full expression in her new love for walking and her deep interest in flowers. Later, she was to use her artistic talents to create pictures from the flowers she dried and pressed – which she exhibited and later gathered into a book. But although all these interests came to mean a lot to her it took time, and in between Grace suffered a series of blows.

The first came in June 1960, when her father died of stomach cancer. Although she had known he was very ill, the impact of Jack's death was tremendous. Grace flew back to Philadelphia for the funeral, and in the middle of grieving she was dealt another blow. Rumours reached her that while she was in mourning Rainier was enjoying himself. He was photographed out dancing with Zenaide, her attractive Spanish lady-in-waiting. Although the story had a perfectly innocent explanation, Grace found it difficult to shrug off. Soon after she came back, she dismissed Zenaide.

As if that were not enough, a few months later, her beloved pet poodle, Oliver, was savaged to death by another dog while they were on a skiing holiday in Switzerland. Oliver had been a present from Cary Grant and his wife after making *To Catch a Thief*.

This succession of unhappy events shook Grace's fragile security, and possibly even her confidence in herself. In addition, she felt increasingly that her very identity was being obliterated. Her longings for her own career, which she had kept to herself since she married

in the vain hope that they would go away, now would not be silenced. In 1962, Hitchcock sent her a stunning script, with a marvellous central role – *Marnie* – and she badly wanted to do it. Rainier, who could not bear to see Grace so unhappy, finally agreed.

Rainier's capitulation was astounding, in view of his past disapproval of Grace's career. He nevertheless issued an announcement to the people of Monaco in March that year, in which they were reassured that filming would be short. A later announcement revealed that all the money Grace earned would go to a charity to help needy children and young athletes in Monaco.

The reaction in Monaco was unanimous outrage. So much so that Grace was forced, reluctantly, to give up the project. She finally made a statement saying she would not be playing the role, because the shooting dates had been changed and because 'I have been very influenced by the reaction which the announcement provoked in Monaco.' She was never to appear on the screen again.

♛ *Story time in the nursery, with Caroline, Albert and Grace's pet poodle, Oliver* above, *was a regular feature at the Palace. Later, when they were older, the children were allowed to travel on their own with their nanny, Maureen King. Prince Albert and Princess Caroline, aged three and four, are shown* above left, *at London Airport on their way to join Grace and Rainier in Ireland in 1961*

This crisis in Grace's life was counterpointed by a crisis in Rainier's dealings with France. In a drive to bring more trade to Monaco, Rainier had been advertising the great tax advantages for companies settling in Monaco, and President de Gaulle finally took action, issuing several ultimatums that threatened the autonomy of Monaco. Finally, compromises were reached that satisfied both sides. But only, some said, because of Grace, who had utterly charmed the President during her state visit to Paris with Rainier in 1957.

With Grace's hopes for a new start in films crushed, she turned to what gave her comfort and what she knew she did well – her role as a mother. Soon she was pregnant again. But, tragically, Grace had a miscarriage on 25 June 1962. On top of that, Madge Tivey-Faucon retired as lady-in-waiting and soon appalled and betrayed her former employers by writing a series of articles about Grace and Rainier.

A series of body blows like this can make or break a marriage, and despite everything Grace was very much in love with her husband, and adored her duties as a mother. But she had finally discovered that it was not enough. In an interview she gave many years later, Grace said, 'During the first years of my marriage I lost my identity because I didn't have ways of recharging my batteries that I had depended on before. I tended to let my husband and his life and work absorb my personality. This was wrong. I had to find ways of finding myself.'

The birth of Stephanie

Before she found the way, however, there were supremely happy moments in her life. On 1 February 1965, Stephanie Marie Elisabeth was born, also at home and without drugs. As the cannon boomed the 21-gun message that a Princess had been born, Albert announced proudly, 'I got 101!'

For a while, life continued much as usual, but as the children grew older, lessons at the Palace became inappropriate. There was no question of sending the children away to school while they were young. Caroline – always the scholar of the family – was placed in a

♔ *Stephanie's arrival completed the family, but time spent with Caroline and Albert was equally important to both parents. Grace, anxious to maintain links with her homeland, took the children on regular visits to the United States. Caroline is shown* top *meeting Mickey Mouse at the 1968 World Fair in New York. As she reached adolescence* centre, *Caroline became more headstrong and Grace had trouble in controlling her growing impetuosity. Rainier, meanwhile, watched over the more placid Albert* above

convent school in Monaco until the age 14, when she was sent to England to continue her education at St Mary's Convent at Ascot.

Albert also went to school in Monaco. His father was certainly keen not to duplicate with his son his own miserable experiences at an English public school. Grace described Albert as 'gentle and shy and very neat and methodical'.

An example of Albert's unchildlike temperament amused his parents. They took him to the circus one day and while the other children watched enthralled, Rainier was baffled to see that his son was more interested in following the programme to see that the acts performed everything in the correct order.

Albert, too, did well at the local school, although unlike Caroline he was not an academic star. He shone in other ways. Athletically he was a Kelly, and his sense of humour was very well developed. In fact, Albert studied in Monaco until he was 16, and was then sent to college in America.

Grace was protective of all her children, but Albert's sweetness tugged at her heart, particularly, as she said, because, 'More is expected of him, and all eyes are on him, waiting for him to make a mistake.'

Another miscarriage

Stephanie was very soon making herself felt as the baby of the family, despite the fact that Grace and Rainier tried hard not to spoil her (although that is sometimes inevitable with the last or longed-for child). She was charming, strong-willed and utterly irrepressible. As Grace commented to friends later, 'I could have beaten her like a gong without making her give way.' What she needed was another child close in age to be her friend, and to take attention away from her. In summer of 1967, Grace was thrilled to find herself pregnant again.

She was nearly four months into her pregnancy when the entire family made the trip to Canada to visit Expo 67. Soon after arriving, Grace and Rainier hosted a reception for Monaco's National Day at the fair, and the next day Grace was taken ill. She was put to bed, and then the pains started. The next day she miscarried yet again. Grace was 38, and privately knew that this had probably been her last chance to have another child.

Grace was proud of the way she had brought her children up, and she had a right to be. Before Caroline went to school in England, they had been particularly close. Grace knew that adolescence, when it came, was a stormy period, but even so, she was unprepared for the controversy ahead.

Hazel Brooke, Reigate

B Bakalian/Frank Spooner

Daniel Simon/Gamma/Frank Spooner

Helton Deutsch Collection

THE MAKING OF MONACO

Grace's arrival in Monaco did much to boost Monaco's image abroad, providing a magnet for the international jet set. Typical high spots in the Monégasque calendar included the Grand Prix, tennis tournaments and a host of gala functions in the world-famous Casino. Despite the formality of some of these occasions, they were not without their moments of unpredictability. The 1966 picture *below right* shows Grace attending a banquet commemorating the Casino's centenary – and carrying an ice cream!

DEATH OF A PRINCESS

AS THE CHILDREN APPROACHED ADULTHOOD, GRACE AND RAINIER PURSUED SEPARATE PRIVATE INTERESTS BEHIND THE FACADE OF A BUSY PUBLIC SCHEDULE. THEN, ONE SUMMER'S DAY, THE FAMILY'S LIVES WERE SHATTERED

GRACE WAS TO REMARK IN 1973, 'Having a teenage daughter is like riding a young horse over an unknown steeplechase. You don't know when to pull up the reins, when to let the horse have its head – or what.' She was already grappling unsuccessfully with an independent young daughter aching to break free.

When she was 16, Caroline insisted on finishing her education in Paris. Her parents were not against the idea, but Grace was worried about her young daughter being exposed to the high life and low press of a glamorous, international capital.

The press went wild. Caroline had never known anything like it before. 'Why do I have to be a Princess?' she raged. Grace felt she could not leave her alone to cope, even if it meant leaving Rainier and Albert behind for months at a time – something Rainier was very much against. But Grace insisted, and she and Stephanie moved into their Paris apartment to watch over Caroline.

With the wisdom of hindsight, Grace knew afterwards that she had done the wrong thing. By the time she was 18, Caroline was revelling in Parisian nightlife and resenting her mother's attempts to make her behave like a demure Princess – or a young Grace Kelly.

New projects
But if her relationships with her children were occasionally fraught, Grace was at last achieving peace within herself, as she found a satisfying way to reconcile her stifled talents with her role as Princess.

Whereas acting in a film would have caused loss of dignity, Grace eventually found that she could be involved with film-making on other levels. The 90-minute documentary, *The Children of Theatre Street*, about a Russian ballet school, had already been made when Grace was approached to do the narration.

In 1976, she agreed to take a seat on the board of the film company, Twentieth Century-Fox. But the projects that gave her the most

As Grace developed her own interests, private moments with Rainier below left *became increasingly rare – something he was not happy about. But Grace blossomed again in the limelight and her poetry readings became a great success. In 1981, she hosted a gala evening in London attended by the recently engaged Prince Charles and Lady Diana Spencer* below

42

THE PRINCESS AND THE PLAYBOY

Caroline married Philippe Junot on 29 June 1978. Brought up behind the strict walls of the Palace, she had been dazzled by the free spirit of this practised playboy, 17 years her senior. Soon, she seemed to fly entirely out of Grace and Rainier's control and gave up plans to study at Princeton. The final straw came when she was photographed nude with Junot at St Tropez. Grace and Rainier were furious, but could do little but agree to the marriage. 'Well, perhaps it's for the better,' Grace observed wryly, 'This way she'll have a successful second marriage.' Caroline was divorced in 1980

pleasure were the poetry readings that gradually came to punctuate her working year.

They started when she was invited to appear at the Edinburgh Festival in 1976. Edinburgh was followed by a Shakespeare reading at Stratford-upon-Avon, and after that, Grace regularly gave readings – travelling to Dublin and Vienna and touring the United States several times.

Rainier was initially annoyed that this new enthusiasm meant that Grace spent so much time on the road. But eventually he became reconciled to her new way of living as he realized that her enthusiasms revived her, and that what she was doing increased her dignity and stature as Princess of Monaco in the eyes of the world.

On a personal level, as his wife rather than as a princess, Rainier could also see how much more fulfilled Grace was, now that she had something of her own, and as this had worried him in the early years, he could only have been pleased with the change in her.

As they matured, Grace and Rainier felt secure enough in their roles to pursue separate leisure interests in the few private moments their busy private schedules allowed – he, on his yacht; she, roaming the Monégasque hills collecting wild flowers to be dried and skilfully arranged in pictures.

A couple leading increasingly independent lives are bound to set off rumours and speculation, but none about Rainier and Grace could be substantiated. Besides, husband and wife also worked together. They oversaw Grace's favourite new venture, the Princess

Grace Theatre. This beautifully restored building was opened on 18 December 1981 with a show that integrated Monaco's three languages: French, Italian and English.

Problems with Stephanie

Grace had continued to spend much of the year in Paris, now supervising Stephanie who was attending school.

In Paris, Grace experienced something of the same troubles with Stephanie that she had with Caroline. But they were not so difficult for Grace to handle the second time around.

Stephanie was also somewhat easier to handle, because there was less of a rivalry in this mother-daughter relationship. But as the school years were drawing to an end, Grace found herself dealing with another lovesick, headstrong daughter. At 16, in the October of 1981, Stephanie had fallen in love with Paul Belmondo, the handsome son of the French film star Jean-Paul Belmondo, just a year older than Stephanie. They soon became inseparable.

Worried about the intensity of Stephanie's feelings, Grace and Rainier insisted that she spend much of the summer of 1982 with them in Monaco or Roc Agel. It was a tiring time for Grace. The exhaustion often showed and she was plagued by minor illnesses. Drinking had also made her put on weight, cleverly disguised in flowing dresses, but it no longer seemed to matter. It was a relief, then, to spend the remainder of the summer at Roc Agel trying to gather strength for the autumn.

The final scene

On 13 September 1982, Grace and Stephanie were ready to leave Roc Agel. Stephanie was going back to Paris to enrol in a course for fashion designers, and Grace was going too,

👑 *In 1981, Grace and Rainier celebrated their silver wedding anniversary in Los Angeles – a happy, intimate gathering at the home of Frank Sinatra, with family and old friends, below. For their next anniversary, they were in Taiwan, where Grace launched a renovated* Constitution *– the ship that had brought her to Monaco as a bride. It was to be their last such celebration*

to keep a maternal eye on her.

Grace filled the back seat of her Rover 3500 with suitcases and dresses and, because of the lack of space, she decided not to involve the chauffeur. They set out at 9.30 am with Grace driving.

As the car pulled on to the dangerous stretch of road with its three particularly sharp hairpin bends, a truck driver came up behind them. He saw that the car in front negotiated the first two bends normally, but just as the last bend was coming up, the car started to zig-zag.

'I don't know what happened,' the truck driver said. 'The corner came up ... I did not see it slow down ...' The car hurtled over 100 feet down the side of the cliff and landed on its side.

Stephanie was helped out and, distraught, begged the people who had gathered to help her mother. The Palace was called, and the hospital.

Grace was unconscious, with bruises, a wound on her scalp and an obviously broken right leg. Rainier and Albert, in deep shock, had gone straight from Roc Agel and were waiting at the hospital in Monaco as the ambulance arrived. Caroline, who was in London, flew back that evening.

While Stephanie was in one ward with injuries to her back being tended, the doctors did what they could for Grace. As the day progressed, she went into a coma, and as the doctors dealt with her external injuries, it was clear that her general condition was worsening. Further tests revealed there was no hope.

Rainier was devastated. Someone else drafted a press release in panic, which gave no hint of the severity of Grace's injuries and, in the absence of hard facts, the statement said that the brakes had failed – which was subsequently found to be untrue.

The next morning, Caroline and Albert went to say their last farewell to their mother. Then Rainier was left alone with Grace. Guided by the doctors, the life support machine was allowed to be switched off. Grace died that night at 10.30 pm.

> ### 'Monte Carlo will always be "Grace's Place" and she will always be deeply missed'
> DIRK BOGARDE

Amid the grief and shock that spread beyond the family and Monaco through the world, there was also intense speculation as to exactly what had happened. The most likely explanation seems to be the one advanced by the doctors – Grace had suffered a mild stroke, which would not have been so serious if it had happened anywhere but on that dangerous road.

Rainier found it hard to come to terms with Grace's death. His grief was no less intense for all the international attention focused on Monaco – almost as much as at the wedding – with celebrities, royalty and newsmen flying in. But this time, it was different – there was no celebration, no hysteria. As Rainier conceded, 'On the day of the funeral, there was no sound in all the principality.'

Grace was laid to rest in the royal vault. The inscription on her marble tomb reads simply, 'Grace Patricia, wife of Rainier III, died the year of our Lord, 1982'.

John Frost

👑 *The treacherous hairpin bends* below, *around which Grace had hurtled with a petrified Cary Grant while filming* To Catch a Thief, *were to claim her life in 1982. The news of her death stunned the world and her sorrowing family* bottom *as they saw Grace off on her last journey*

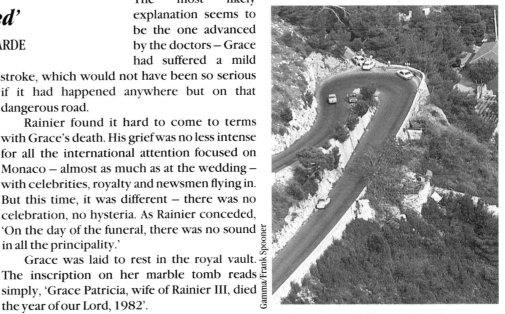

Gamma/Frank Spooner

Pierre Perrin/Gamma/Frank Spooner

PRINCESS GRACE 1929-1982

Ever in the spotlight, Grace Kelly was the living embodiment of the American Dream. But throughout this glamorous public life, there were also moments of intense private happiness. From memories of a simple childhood to winning the Oscar, from her engagement and marriage to Rainier to the birth of her children – each was to hold a special place in her heart

Bulletin/Temple Urban Archives

♛ Grace preserved her birthday for ever in the cement outside the front door of her Philadelphia home

Rex Features

THURSDAY, NOVEMBER 17, 1949

Bulletin/Temple Urban Archives

'THE FATHER': Raymond Massey, as the tormented father, listens as his wife, played by Mady Christians, dictatorially reveals her plans for their daughter, Bertha, played by Grace Kelly. 'Bertha is to leave home. Bertha is to go to boarding school in the city. She leaves in two weeks.' The August Strindberg drama opened last night at the Cort Theater.

November 16, 1949. The cast:
A Captain of Cavalry___Raymond Massey
A Soldier_____Charles Snyder
The Pastor_____Philip Huston
Another Soldier_____Paul Larson
The Captain's Wife____Mady Christians
The Doctor_____John D. Seymour
The Nurse_____Mary Morris
The Captain's Daughter___Grace Kelly

of her soldier-scientist husband. There is good work from players in the quieter roles—from John D. Seymour as the doctor, Philip Huston as the pastor, Mary Morris as the old and grieving nurse and Charles Snyder as a soldier. Grace Kelly, in the part of the daughter, makes a thoroughly impressive Broadway debut.

Raymond Massey has given skillful direction to the production of Richard W. Krakeur and Robert L. Joseph, but "The Father," for all of its standing in the

Bulletin/Temple Urban Archives

♛ Grace never wanted to forget her career as an actress, from her first Broadway role, *top left* in Strindberg's play *The Father*, to the supreme accolade *left* – winning an Oscar for *The Country Girl*

♛ Grace's pet poodle, Oliver, was always part of the family. A gift from Cary Grant after filming *To Catch A Thief*, Oliver came to represent her one enduring link with the United States

Jack Albins/Pictorial Parade

Syndication International

Sygma/John Hillelson

Topham Picture Library

♔ A radiant Grace exults over baby Caroline. Private moments caught fleetingly, such as this and an all-too-rare stroll through the Palace gardens with Rainier, were prized dearly

♔ A delighted Grace and Rainier announced their engagement to the world on 5 January 1956 in Philadelphia. Grace had earlier shown the engagement ring to her sceptical parents as a 'friendship' ring. But they knew that the diamonds and rubies entwined to reflect the colours of Monaco meant more. And, of course, it fitted perfectly

EPILOGUE

Grace's death left a void not only in Monaco's public life, but also, it seemed at the time, a sadly irreparable one in her family. But if, formerly, she had to struggle to keep the family united, after her death her children soon seemed to acquire a maturity born of their suffering.

Stephanie, who had been the 'baby' of the family, developed into a spectacular beauty, and she was, briefly, a highly successful model.

Albert was the one child most like Grace. It is said that Rainier did not wish him to have the same problems he had of not having a role and responsibility until both were suddenly thrust upon him.

The one whose life changed most radically was Caroline. Far too intelligent not to learn from her mistakes, she 'sobered up' considerably after her divorce. It is she who is 'first lady' in Monaco, taking on most of her mother's official duties and working closely with Rainier. In late 1983, she was married again, to a rich young Italian, Stefano Casiraghi.

The dream ends

Grace and Rainier had spent 26 years together. There had been, as with most marriages, years of happiness and fulfilment, disappointments and tensions. Theirs was not an easy life to play out before inquisitive public scrutiny, but they had a deep commitment to their marriage, which sprang from their need to create the happy family life both had missed as children.

The little girl who had fantasized about being a princess and the lonely little boy who had made her one had achieved what the whole world wants to believe in — a fairytale come true.

♛ *Without Grace, the family had to pick up the threads of their lives individually. Rainier retreated for a while into the country, hunting. The children, bereft of the strong, cohesive influence of their mother, shouldered adult responsibilities, evaded so far. Albert and Caroline provided support to the grief-stricken Rainier, while he in turn was looked to most by the youngest, Stephanie. Gradually, the wounds healed and the family adjusted to new lives ahead*